Dominick Argento

Three Meditations

Solo Soprano

HENDON MUSIC

BOOSEY & HAWKES

AN IMAGEM COMPANY

DISTRIBUTED BY

HAL•LEONARD®
CORPORATION
7777 W. BLUEMOUND RD. P.O. BOX 13819 MILWAUKEE, WI 53213

www.boosey.com
www.halleonard.com

First performed on June 11, 2008
at James J. Hill House, Saint Paul, MN
by Maria Jett, soprano

Duration: 6 ½ minutes

THE LAST INVOCATION
By Walt Whitman

At the last, tenderly,
From the walls of the powerful fortress'd house,
From the clasp of the knitted locks, from the keep of the well-closed doors,
Let me be wafted.

Let me glide noiselessly forth;
With the key of softness unlock the locks--with a whisper,
Set ope the doors O soul.

Tenderly--be not impatient,
(Strong is your hold O mortal flesh,
Strong is your hold O love.)

SILVER
By Walter de la Mare

Slowly, silently, now the moon
Walks the night in her silver shoon;
This way, and that, she peers, and sees
Silver fruit upon silver trees;
One by one the casements catch
Her beams beneath the silvery thatch;
Couched in his kennel, like a log,
With paws of silver sleeps the dog;
From their shadowy cote the white breasts peep
Of doves in silver feathered sleep
A harvest mouse goes scampering by,
With silver claws, and silver eye;
And moveless fish in the water gleam,
By silver reeds in a silver stream.

DEEP IS THE HEART OF THE LAKE
By Alun Lewis

Deep is the heart of the lake where the last light is clinging
A strange foreboding voice is patiently singing
Do not fear to venture where the last light trembles
Because you were in love. Love never dissembles.
Fear not more the boast, the bully, the lies, the vain labor.
Make no show for death as for a rich neighbor.
What stays of the great religions?
An old priest, an old birth.
What stays of the great battles?
Dust on earth.
Cold is the lake water
And dark as history.
Hurry not and fear not this oldest mystery.
This strange voice singing
The slow deep drag of the lake,
This yearning, yearning,
This ending of the heart and its ache.

for Maria Jette, con grazie

Three Meditations
for solo soprano

I. The Last Invocation

**text by
Walt Whitman**

**music by
Dominick Argento**

1'45"

II. Silver

text by
Walter de la Mare

music by
Dominick Argento

III. Deep is the Heart of the Lake

text by
Alun Lewis

music by
Dominick Argento

Deep___ is the heart of the lake___ Where the last light is cling - ing_____ A strange fore - bod - ing voice___ Is pa-tient-ly sing - - - ing.___ Do___ not fear to ven - ture___ Where the last light trem - bles_____ Be - cause you were in love. Love_____ ne - ver dis - sem-bles. Fear not more the boast. the bul-ly,___ The lies, the vain la-bor. Make___ no show for death___ As for a rich neigh-bor.___ What stays___ of the great re-

lig-ions?_____ An old priest, an old birth._____

What stays_____ of the great bat-tles?_____ Dust on earth.

Cold_____ is the lake wa-ter_____ And dark_____ as

hi-sto-ry._____ Hur-ry not and fear not This old-est

my-ster-y._____ (bocca chiusa) _____

This strange voice sing-ing_____ The slow deep drag of the lake,_____

_ This yearn-ing,_____ yearn - - - ing,_____ this

end - ing Of the heart_____ and its ache.

3'10"